THE LIZARD LIBRARY™

The Chameleon

Jake Miller

The Rosen Publishing Group's
PowerKids Press™
New York

Published in 2003 by The Rosen Publishing Group, Inc.
29 East 21st Street, New York, NY 10010

First Edition

Editor: Nancy MacDonell Smith
Book Design: Maria E. Melendez
Book Layout: Eric DePalo

Photo Credits: Cover and title page © Wolfgang Kaehler/CORBIS; p. 4 © Joe McDonald/Animals Animals; p. 6 © Wildlife Pictures/Peter Arnold, Inc.; pp. 7, 16 © Kevin Schafer/CORBIS; pp. 8, 17 © Patti Murray/Animals Animals; p. 11 © Michael & Patricia Fogden/CORBIS; p. 12 © David A. Northcott/CORBIS; p. 15 © Jim Zuckerman/CORBIS; p. 19 © A. Visage/BIOS/Peter Arnold, Inc.; p. 20 (owl) © Digital Vision; p. 20 (chameleon) © R. Andrew Odum/Peter Arnold, Inc.; p. 22 © A. & J. Visage/Peter Arnold, Inc.; border images © Digital Vision.

Miller, Jake, 1969–
The chameleon / Jake Miller.— 1st ed.
     p. cm. — (The Lizard library)
Summary: Describes the life cycle, habitats, and behavior of the chameleon.
Includes bibliographical references (p.   ).
  ISBN 0-8239-6417-5 (lib. bdg.)
1. Chameleons—Juvenile literature. [1. Chameleons.] I. Title.
  QL666.L23 M56 2003
  597.95'6—dc21

                                                                                    2002000095

Manufactured in the United States of America

Contents

A chameleon's tongue is 1 ½ times as long as its body!

What Makes Chameleons Special

The chameleon is a type of lizard that is best known for its ability to change colors. There are chameleons that can change from dark brown or green to bright colors such as purple or red. Not all chameleons are good at changing colors, but they all do have some amazing things in common. All chameleons have eyes that can twist and turn on their own. One eye can be looking straight back while the other eye is looking straight ahead. Chameleons' eyes can also work together so that chameleons have **three-dimensional** vision. They can easily tell how far away something is. They are the only animals in the world that can do all of those different things with their eyes. All chameleons also have very long tongues, which they can shoot out of their mouths to catch insects and other **prey**. A 20-inch (51-cm) veiled chameleon has a 30-inch (76-cm) tongue.

So Many
Different Chameleons

Though they all have long tongues and three-dimensional vision, one kind of chameleon can look very different from another. Some chameleons are only 1 inch (2.5 cm) long. There are also big ones such as the Parson's chameleon. It can grow to be nearly 2 ½ feet (76 cm) long. Chameleons are found in Africa, Spain, Arabia, and India. Many **species** are found only on the island of Madagascar, off the coast of Africa. They live in rainy jungles and in dry deserts. They live down by the sea and high up in the mountains. Some have horns or spines on their heads, and some do not. Most chameleons lay eggs, but some have babies that are born live.

Most chameleons can change color, but some cannot.

Some chameleons have feet that are good for walking on sand.
Other chameleons, like this one, have feet that are good for
holding onto tree branches.

Tree-dwelling chameleons are usually the same color as the leaves or the bark of the trees in which they live. Scientists aren't sure if chameleons use their brains to control color changes or if the changes happen naturally.

Up a Tree
or Down in the Desert

Some chameleons, including one kind from Madagascar known as the jungle panther, live mostly in trees. They have long tails that they can use to hold onto branches while they are sitting high above the ground. The **namaqua** chameleon lives on the ground in the Namib Desert in Africa. It has **adapted** to the great changes in **temperature** that happen there every day. A namaqua chameleon keeps its body temperature between 60°F and 105°F (16°C–41°C), while the temperature of the air goes from near 32°F to 150°F (0°C–66°C). In the morning, when the weather is cool, the chameleon sits in the sun and changes its skin to a dark purple color, because dark colors absorb more sunlight. As soon as it has warmed its body, it changes to a pink color to match the color of the desert sand so that it will be harder for its enemies to see.

I See You, but You Can't See Me

The best defense a chameleon has against its enemies is **camouflage**. The normal color of most chameleons is a perfect match with the color of the places where they spend most of their time. They have other tricks that help them to seem invisible. Chameleons who live in trees have long, flat bodies that are shaped almost like leaves. They sit very still in the trees. They wait until the wind blows before they move, and then they **sway** from side to side when they walk. They look just like leaves blowing in the wind. They walk very slowly, less than ¼ mile per hour (0.4 km/h). This helps them to stay hidden. It also helps that they can move their eyes without moving their bodies or their heads. They can look around for prey, or for **predators** who might want to eat them, without attracting attention.

This chameleon is green and flat. From a distance, it looks like a leaf.

Chameleons change color when they are scared or nervous. Male chameleons change color when they want to impress a female or to scare away other males.

Why and How Chameleons Change Color

Many people think that chameleons change color to match the background against which they are standing. That's not exactly true. A chameleon's normal color is a good match for the place where it spends most of its time. The colors a chameleon can turn are usually very bright, and not a good match for anything around it. The top layer of a chameleon's skin is see-through. Under the top layer are special **cells** that contain different colors. There are red, yellow, blue, and brown cells. When a chameleon changes color, it squeezes some of the cells and makes them smaller. This lets other cells get bigger. For example, if the yellow and blue cells are big and the other cells are small, the chameleon will look green. If the chameleon squeezes out the yellow cells and makes the red ones bigger, it will look purple.

Chameleon Social Life

Male chameleons like to live away from other males. If a male chameleon sees another male of its own species, it will challenge him to a fight. Before they fight, they have to make sure they are members of the same species. Many chameleon species that live near one another look a lot alike. Chameleons can recognize one another by the way their heads look. When a male chameleon recognizes another male of his species, the two will usually fight. First they turn bright colors. Chameleons are very slow moving, so these fights are usually not very dangerous for them. However, in some species, such as the jungle panther, the winner may kill the loser. Fighting chameleons push each other around to see who is the strongest, and they may bite each other. When the loser is ready to quit, he usually turns back to his normal, dull color to show that he gives up.

One big difference between similar species is the shape of their heads. Some species of chameleon have little horns decorating their heads, and others have no decoration at all.

Baby chameleons are about the size of your fingernail. Predators sometimes eat little chameleons. Chameleons have to look after themselves as soon as they hatch.

Baby Chameleons

Chameleons have different ways of having babies. Most chameleons lay eggs. The female Parson's chameleon digs a deep nest in moist soil. She lays between 30 and 60 eggs in the bottom of the nest. The eggs are soft, like leather. The eggs take in water from the soil. Once the babies hatch, they have to dig their way out of the nest.

A Jackson's three-horned chameleon doesn't dig a nest. She carries between 5 and 50 eggs inside her body. The babies develop inside the eggs. When the babies are ready to be born, she lays the eggs on a tree branch. The baby chameleons hatch right away.

Some chameleons hatch in trees instead of under ground.

A Surprising Tongue

Chameleons are expert hunters. Chameleons use their tongues to catch insects and other animals. When a chameleon is hunting, it follows its prey with both eyes. When it is aiming its tongue, a chameleon looks a little cross-eyed. It is making sure it gets the distance right. It can stick its long tongue out fast enough to catch a fly in midair. The end of a chameleon's tongue is covered in a rough pad that feels like sandpaper, and with sticky **saliva**. The pad and the saliva work together to grab whatever the tongue hits. For a long time scientists were confused about how chameleons' tongues worked. Some thought chameleons inflated their tongues with air, like giant balloons. The truth is that chameleons' tongues work in the same way that ours do. **Muscles** squeeze to push the tongue out and to pull it back into the mouth.

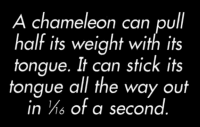

A chameleon can pull half its weight with its tongue. It can stick its tongue all the way out in $\frac{1}{16}$ of a second.

Danger in the Wild

Although they are great hunters, chameleons are not very good at defending themselves. If they are spotted by one of their enemies, chameleons move too slowly to run away, and there is little that they can do to fight back. They don't have sharp claws, dangerous teeth, or any other defenses. Chameleons have many natural enemies. Rats, birds, snakes, and other lizards all like to eat chameleons. Even spiders and ants can eat tiny baby chameleons. Humans also **threaten** chameleons. In some places, humans are building farms and towns on land where chameleons live. Because all the different kinds of chameleons have adapted to live in very specific places, losing just a little piece of **habitat** might cause a whole species to become **extinct**. Another danger to chameleons is being caught and sold as pets.

Owls can easily swoop down on chameleons, because chameleons move too slowly to hide.

21

Chameleons as Pets

Sadly, it is very hard to keep a pet chameleon healthy. Often a chameleon that is for sale in a pet store is already sick. It was probably captured on the other side of the world, and the journey to the store may have been very hard on it. When someone buys a chameleon and brings it home, it often dies very soon. The best kind of chameleon to have as a pet is one that was born in **captivity** and raised to be a pet. Even if you get a healthy chameleon, caring for it can be hard. To keep a chameleon healthy, you have to make its home in your home as close as possible to its home in the wild. The best way for humans to continue to enjoy chameleons is to leave them in their own habitat.

Chameleons need a special diet to stay healthy.

Glossary

adapted (uh-DAP-tid) Changed to fit new conditions.

camouflage (KA-muh-flaj) Something that is colored and patterned to look like its surroundings, so it is hard to see.

captivity (kap-TIH-vih-tee) When a wild animal lives with humans, in a home, on a farm, or in a zoo and not in the wild.

cells (SELZ) Many tiny units that make up all living things.

extinct (ek-STINKT) No longer existing.

habitat (HA-bih-tat) The surroundings where an animal or a plant naturally lives.

muscles (MUH-sulz) Parts of the body underneath the skin that can be tightened or loosened to make the body move.

namaqua (nuh-MAH-kwuh) A species of chameleon that lives in the Namib Desert.

predators (PREH-duh-terz) Animals that kill other animals for food.

prey (PRAY) An animal that is hunted by another animal for food.

saliva (suh-LY-vuh) The liquid in the mouth, sometimes called spit.

species (SPEE-sheez) A single kind of plant or animal. For example, all people are one species.

sway (SWAY) To swing smoothly from side to side.

temperature (TEM-pruh-cher) How hot or cold something is.

threaten (THREH-tin) To be put in danger.

three-dimensional (THREE dih-MEN-shuh-nul) Having height, width, and depth. A flat picture, such as a photograph, is two-dimensional. A sculpture is three-dimensional.

Index

Web Sites

Due to the changing nature of Internet links, PowerKids Press has developed an online list of Web sites related to the subject of this book. This site is updated regularly. Please use this link to access the list:

www.powerkidslinks.com/ll/chamel/